To Mom
— G.M.

Bless the editors
— S.W.

ISBN 978-0-439-23505-1

Printed in China

A Child's Good Night Prayer

by Grace Maccarone
Illustrated by Sam Williams

SCHOLASTIC INC.

New York Toronto London Auckland Sydney Mexico City New Delhi Hong Kong

Bless the moon

Bless the stars

Bless my night-light

Bless my cars

Bless my trucks

Bless my chairs

Bless my table

Bless my bears

Bless my bunny

Bless my mouse

Bless the family
in its house

Bless my pillow

Bless my bed

Bless me, too,
from toes to head

Bless the water,
earth, and air

Bless the children

everywhere

Bless the moon
Bless the stars
Bless my night-light
Bless my cars

Bless my trucks
Bless my chairs
Bless my table
Bless my bears

Bless my bunny
Bless my mouse
Bless the family
in its house

Bless my pillow
Bless my bed
Bless me, too,
from toes to head

Bless the water,
earth, and air
Bless the children
everywhere